How to Start a Business

With Very Little Money

Entrepreneur Series

Saad Ghafoor

Mendon Cottage Books

JD-Biz Publishing

Disclaimer

The information is this book is provided for informational purposes only. It is not intended to be used and medical advice or a substitute for proper medical treatment by a qualified health care provider. The information is believed to be accurate as presented based on research by the author.

The contents have not been evaluated by the U.S. Food and Drug Administration or any other Government or Health Organization and the contents in this book are not to be used to treat cure or prevent disease.

The author or publisher is not responsible for the use or safety of any diet, procedure or treatment mentioned in this book. The author or publisher is not responsible for errors or omissions that may exist.

Warning

The Book is for informational purposes only and before taking on any diet, treatment or medical procedure, it is recommended to consult with your primary health care provider.

Our books are available at

1. Amazon.com
2. *Barnes and Noble*
3. Itunes
4. Kobo
5. Smashwords
6. Google Play Books

Table of Contents

1. Introduction

This book provides information and some useful tips for establishing a business, even for those who have very little investment initially. We will also tell the new comers at business, how to manage enough finance without having to ask a bank for loans. The chapters included in the book will separately cover the components of a business; starting from the concept to cash. The book provides an insight to useful homework that requires being done before a person can establish a functional business for an initial investment as low as $1000. In the chapters that are yet to come, you will figure out the difference between the decisions that can prove to be makers or breakers of your business idea.

2. Choosing a Line of Business

It is very important, to first of all, pin point what your business would actually do. A business can be oriented in two directions; either service based or product based. Service based businesses include those activities that require a specific skill.

Initial Options:

For people with only a little investment to start with, service-based business is usually a better option, as the entrepreneur will be using his/her own skills and knowledge of the business to implement the theory into practical results. However, there are product-based opportunities which can be started with a low investment as well.

Which path to take
© Klekta Darya - Fotolia.com

Whichever business type is decided, the next order of thinking should be on whether a particular idea, which has been thought through, is going to be implemented, or if a person wants to establish a business which is currently being operated in the market by other businessmen. A novel idea of a business, which has never been in the market before, consists of huge rewards if successful, but at the same time incorporates massive risks as well. Initial options should be based on this decision, because it will have a titanic impact on the success or failure of the business. Obviously, if your own idea is good enough to jump through the obstacles with significant results, pursuing it will be the best option, but the question arises if it is really good enough to stand and fight against the world of competition. The answer can be found with deep research of the idea to find out whether the market can handle the level of intellectuality in it. Talking to friends and family will help you to acknowledge whether people would really want to buy your product or utilize the service that you'll be providing.

The other option to go for is an established line of business and opening a franchise. There are a few advantages and disadvantages on the plate, like any other business type. Since many entrepreneurs might already be progressing with their business, details of their open strategies of how they started and where they stand on the market success today will be easily accessible and apparent. Disadvantages lie on the stance of competition which however, can be overcome if the product in mind or the service offered is given with an edge of differentiation.

The way of deciding is to look upon what grasps your interest the most and largely holds the enthusiasm. Entrepreneurs have to dedicate a lot of time to their own business, because starting from scratch and building an empire of triumph is not a simple chutes and ladders game. Since so much dedication and commitment is required, if the concept of the product or service that you're offering doesn't hold your interest, it is hardly possible that you'll be able to instill, in a customer, the level of interest required to attract them towards your product.

Overall, the initial options lie on the basis of the basic idea of differentiation as to what you can provide to a market. Either chose a novel idea of your own or if you're choosing an established line of business, you must have something in mind that differentiates you from all the other developed business of the same industry.

Feasibility Studies of Alternatives:

There are millions of options to choose from when it comes to selecting a business type, but only a few of them will be the right one for you. Once you have analyzed the initial options, narrowing down an industry will be next. Since we are focusing on little investment to start with, this will instantly cut out many options like a restaurant business, a telecom business, etc.

Choosing the business that fits your box of expertise and resources is essential and thus the initial needs of a business has to be evaluated. For example, if one decides to start an event planning business then the requirements are mainly good networking, a computer for online marketing, and a website. All these would cost much less than $1000 and the entrepreneur is good to go. Whereas if someone is willing to develop an automobile business, it is an impossible scenario as the investment required in the essentials, such as machinery, is not even moderate enough to consider.

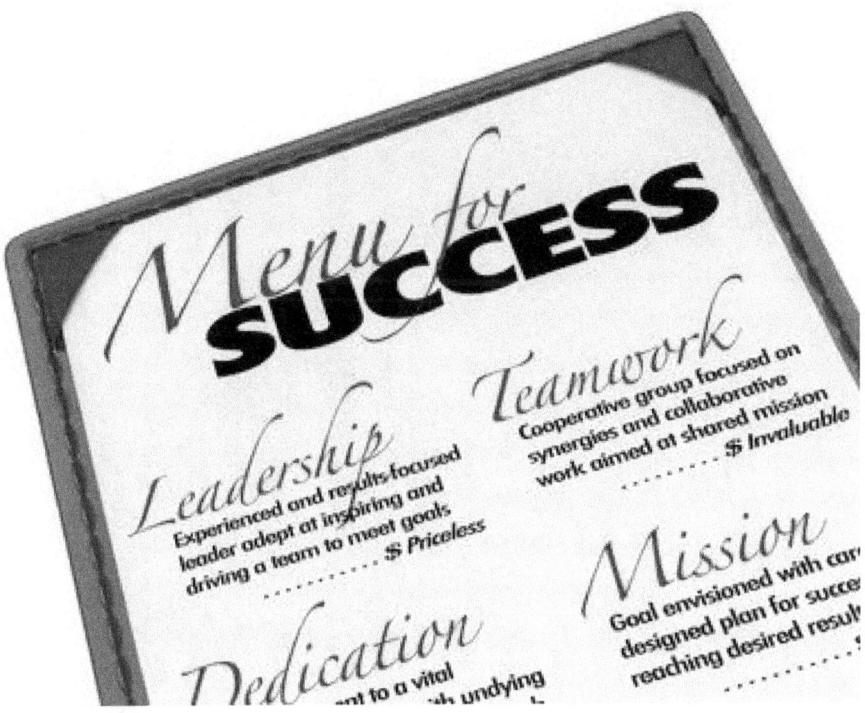

Menu for Success Order Your Results Goal Victory
© *iQoncept - Fotolia.com*

Selecting a business that requires an office will cost a huge amount therefore alternatives should be thought about. For example, you might have a garage out of use or even a study area which can be renovated to make a small, but ample size room to set up your things. Such a business might be a salon or clothing store business, both of which require a definite space to work in.

Competition is a fundamental threat to consider around your business industry. After you narrow down your options, you will need to do additional research to figure out how strong the competition is. You also want to find out how many other businesses like yours are around the area. If so, then alternative business options should be evaluated. However, if you truly believe that what you'll be providing to your customers is far better than that of your competitors, success might just follow you throughout.

Finalizing the Choice:

With all the research work being done, it is important to remain focused on the objectives of your own. Once you're finished with your highly tedious research work, you'll realize that your knowledge about many industries has widened. This allows a person to properly evaluate all the alternatives and choose the business line that will work best for them at that moment; a business that fits their criteria of interest, expertise, and investment.

3. Formation of a Business Plan

Definition of the Business Activities:

Business activities help to get in line with the operations of the entire business. It encompasses the definition of the kinds of activities that you'll be performing at each stage of the business. There are different paths in one business and you will have to choose the path which will then define what your business is really about. In doing this it will exemplify the mission and vision of the business. A company's mission is the ultimate tool of character and operation depiction of the business in the course of which it is able to distinguish itself from its competitors of the marketplace.

What will be your core operation of the business in which you will eventually see your profit generating from? Is it the production, selling, shipping, or any other operation pertaining to what you have in mind for your business? For example, if you have a bakery of your own, will you be buying your bakery products or will you produce them on your own? Will you sell them to the customers directly or will your business include only in producing them and selling them to wholesalers. Services such as the shipment of bakery products to the doorstep might also be a viable operation. This will give you on overall picture of the operating costs of your business, which by the way, is the most critical part and the objective should always be to keep them to a minimal amount.

Overall, it is on you to decide and define the core activities of your business. What you choose to put into action will ultimately generate your profit. You will need to mention the effective goals of the business that you wish to foresee in the future, and how you decide to function in order to achieve them. The reason for identifying such operations clearly and writing them out is to always have a focus on what the prime responsibilities are, and for avoiding a tilt into operations that might incur less profit than other operations.

word cloud - strategic planning
© *z_amir - Fotolia.com*

Incorporate the functions of each level of staff, from the beginning, into the business plan so that everyone acknowledges their own responsibility towards the business. It might not be possible to hire employees with little investment from the start, but as the business grows, you will want to fine-tune them and that is only possible when there are no blurred lines on the responsibility aspect of the operations.

In order to have a large business in the future, a crystal clear idea of the fundamental operations of the business is very essential as shareholders or investors look for such details to ensure that the business is viable and profitable. Also, all the big features of the business that you think will be the leading factors to the success should be noted and written down to maximize the confidence of the partners, if any, or future investors of your business.

Strategic Management Process:

The definition of the business activities lays out the goals of the business, but a more important aim is to critically lay out the strategy of the business. This will be followed throughout in order to accomplish its desired mission, objectives, and goals. It describes the lefts and rights through which your business will arrive at its destination with the maximum positive result i.e. maximum profits.

How? Formulating the strategy of a business means to illustrate how the strengths of the business will contribute and overcome the business's weaknesses in providing the product or service that you have decided to market. There are analytical and descriptive tools to help with the strategic management process and to compare your business to others of the same industry. People usually ask why and when does the need of a strategic management process even arise and the simplest answer is the link to the "competitive advantage". The competitive advantage is the additional advantage a company has over its competitors that is gained by differentiating the product or service from all other business firms of the same industry.

SWOT analysis is the tool of perfection in analyzing the strategies that are to be pursued by a business. It is a methodology, scrutinizing the prospective strategies of a company by amalgamation of an organization's strengths, weaknesses, opportunities, and threats (SWOT). Strengths and weaknesses include the internal factors that alter the course of action of the business. Strengths act as the enzyme which elevates the chances of effective execution of a mission, objectives, and goals whereas the weaknesses contribute as hurdles on the pathway of the same accomplishment. Opportunities and threats incorporate the external factors, macro-environment, that alters the company's ability to achieve its mission, objectives, and goals. Opportunities give rise to pathways through which a company can effectively undergo its action of turning a mission into reality and threats acts as negative factors, or speed breakers on the pathway, which are too be realized and passed through shrewdly.

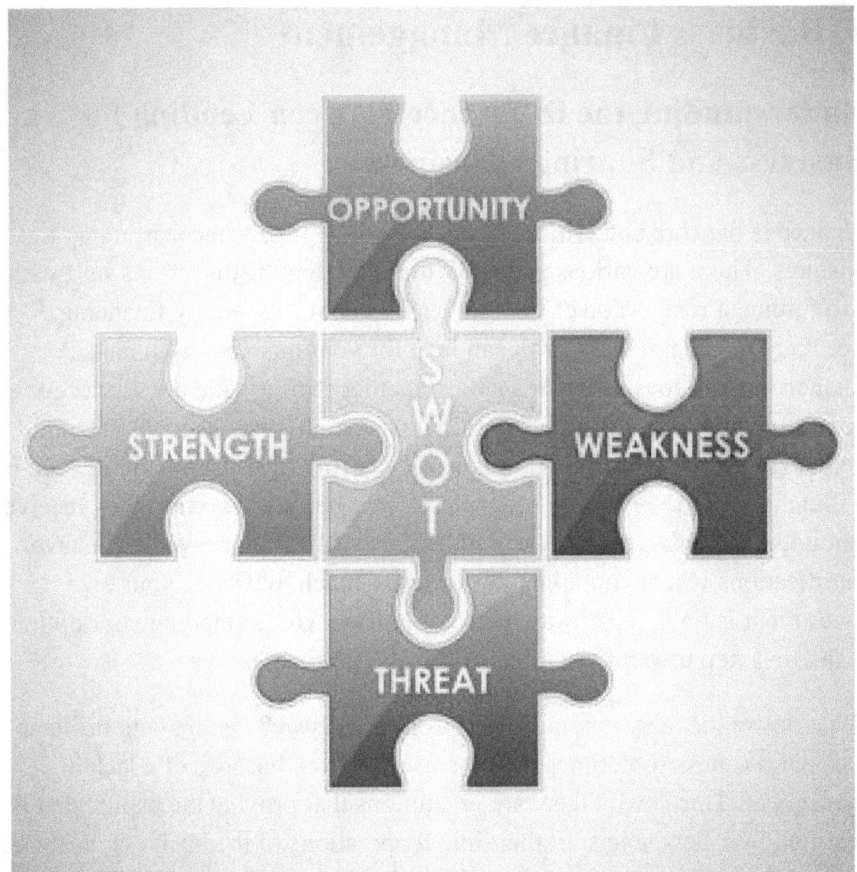

SWOT Analysis
© *vectomart - Fotolia.com*

By using this methodology, strategies can be articulated and those strategies will ensure that you have met the criteria of determining and addressing the core and critical issues of your business. This brainstorming process is very imperative to the business and thus help could be taken from other related people for greater efficiency.

4. Business Finance Management

Understanding the Difference between Lending for a Business and Sharing a Business:

Finance is the core and critical matter to contemplate when starting up a business. There are various pathways to travel, but the diversions start with two foremost roads. You can opt either for debt or for equity financing. Speaking in general terms, you can lend for your business from banks, financial institutions, or other such companies that provide the service, or you can simply share your business. The question arises as to why would people go through the mind-numbing process of acquiring a loan, or even be willing to share their profits with others? It is because in return they receive amounts, or capital, for investing into their business. However, both have ramifications which you might not venerate much, but since your own investment is tight, a pathway has to be chosen. Understanding your options is the first step towards your decision-making process.

What do we mean by lending for a business anyway? People with brilliant ideas of business sometimes hold themselves back because of a lack of investment. This is why there are institutions that provide the capital that is required by a person to start their initial operations of the business. With the help of the loan, you can start whichever business you think has the potential to stand out and shine. Hopes and dreams of many people have been translated into reality with the help of such loans, and this is why the concept has grown so rapidly. In this world, there are no free tickets to heaven. If you are a strict aficionado of sole proprietorship, lending is the best suitable option available. Such institutions charge interest amounts on the investment loaned to the entrepreneur and it might be low or high depending upon the policies of body providing the loan. The dilemma that arises when procuring loans is that they ask for collateral which is only on the basis of assets. After that, they decide whether one deserves the loan or not. Any institution would take back all the collateral put on hold if you're unable to pay the interest amounts regularly, thus putting all your assets at high risk. Fulfilling the prerequisites of institution, banks especially, can be a relentless and daunting process. The banks also have the right to then imply tight restrictions on the policies such as keeping the debt-to-equity ratio at a certain level or below, and if you're unable to do so, the bank will instantly ask you to repay the loan no matter what your situation. The terms and payments agreed over on the loan always include the obligation towards delivering the interest payments at all times. Banks are not concerned towards the success or failure of your business as long as they are receiving their interest amounts. Moreover, it also confines the business into an inflexibility zone, where they do not get much opportunity to use their profits to enhance their business.

Approved loan application form and dollar bills
© mangostock - Fotolia.com

A stock is principally a share of your business that you sell to someone, and in the process, that person becomes entitled to the ownership of your business. The implication being, that all the assets and earnings of the business then has to be shared with the person acquiring a stock in your business. If you're willing to sell parts of your business to someone, you ought to receive something in return. In this case, it is the capital that you need to bring the business on track of competition. The greater the number of stocks acquired by an individual, the ownership stake becomes more prominent. A person, even after the attainment of stocks, has absolutely no say in how to run the business, depicting that all the strategic decisions and implementation will depend on you. The greatest advantage of selling stocks is that the dividends are to be paid to the shareholders, with the conditions being that the business generates profit. Loss of the company means loss for the shareholders unlike in loans, where banks or institutions are in no concern with profits or losses of the business. Large multinational corporations and small businesses offer their stocks on the market and raise capital for the company. Also, equity financing doesn't require any interference of interest amounts, which can become an entrepreneurs' worst nightmare. However, convincing an investor to invest in your business can be very difficult and they might patronize you with hundreds of questions. But, if you're able to crack a deal, you are good to go for the running of your business.

Business Icons © *Rudie - Fotolia.com*

Stressing your mind with which financing to use can be very tedious. Thus, remembering a few lines of intellect while making the decision can reduce the pressure. You have gone through the difference between debt financing and equity financing and their pros and cons, so keeping all of that in mind, which one do you think is more suitable for you? Can you afford to pay the interest amount to the institution from which you have acquired the loan? Can you convince investors to buy stocks of your company? For businesses that require a heavy investment, procuring a loan might not be a feasible idea. For example, if you want to enhance your restaurant business, $1000 is highly insufficient because you would need a rental place, equipment, chefs, etc., all of which are high quality expenses. Now, if you opt for lending for your business, such a large investment would mean a higher interest amount with the principal payment. How does that sound to you? Not alluring, I suppose. In businesses like these, it is always better to share your business i.e. go for equity financing.

Now for example, if you are operating a consulting service business, lending would definitely work better for you. Why? Because in service-based business, your knowledge and skills are the ultimate tools through which you can provide your customer with the sheer enormity of experience. All you might need is a few employees to start working with, a rental place, and maybe few other things. Low requirements always make lending a superior option.

5. Workforce Management

Understanding Effective Recruitment:

Human resource management can include a wide range of staff. In a small business, entrepreneurs are more focused and committed in earning profits that they forget the hidden momentous part which assists highly in the success of a business. The secret is to hire the best employee at the most affordable rates. The mission is to improve the organizational performance, and the culture created by employees greatly impacts it. The word effecting is used in the sense that employees only with competencies, good social, and communication skills, personal attributes, etc. should be hired in order to enhance the value of your business. The importance of effective recruitments comes under the mistakes that can be made if you hire the wrong people whose skills are of absolutely no use to you. A high turnover rate creates a bad impression of your business and can lead to the low morale of other employees. With little investment in our hand, you only have the credibility to hire a few employees, but those you do hire should be fully capable of addressing the business intellectually. You cannot afford to give them training experience and carry on with your business work afterwards, as that would just waste your precious resources; mainly time and money. You'll have no room for such oversights as you're already in a taut situation. Always remember, hire the right people for effective teamwork and that is what will help you to flow though the right track flawlessly.

Screening out Efficient and Effective Employees:

There is always a systematic way of carrying out a function of such utter importance. Addressing issues and brainstorming the possible advantages an employee can contribute to your organization is a good way to start with the recruitment. Professionalism is the fundamental prospect that you should be looking for in an employee, as only then only will he/she be taken seriously. For screening out the most efficient and competent employee, going through their CV is just not enough. It is advisable to call in the potential employees for an interview and ask them several questions about their education, experience, and background. Assess the candidates with scrutiny by noting their behavior towards the job description and notice how enthusiastic they are about the job. A list of questions can be prepared beforehand that you think are the most relevant to the job being displayed. Long interviews help to better evaluate a candidate thoroughly and since you will be giving the candidate a job, there is no need for shyness in asking too many questions that you think are relevant.

Talent management in word tag cloud
© Rafal Olechowski - Fotolia.com

Performance Management and its Importance:

Performance management is a cutter Human resource activity (HR) which encompasses the factors concerned with the employee of an organization or company. The concept of such management developed due to many factors relating to the failure of a business, because of incompetent and unmotivated employees. Employees are a vital part of your business and keeping them on track is the responsibility of the general manager. In organizations that have a few managerial levels, the control over the employees is wider than that of higher management levels. Performance management consists of work such as tracking performances of employees, goal setting, training and development programs, consistent progress review, feedback, and consequently rewarding the achievers. All of these things provide the platform through which an organization can opt for its better performance. By taking individual employees into consideration and improving their performances within a comprehensive framework, a superior performance level is achieved throughout the organization, enabling the utilization of the employee potential to a maximum.

training and development concepts
© *Viorel Sima - Fotolia.com*

How you nourish your employees, with norms, core values, and activities, will define the competency and productivity of your business. This is the ultimate reason as to why performance management is highly impertinent. Employees need to feel a part of your company, be seen and appreciated. Keep your employees happy and they will keep your customers satisfied in return. The culture is developed by the leaders and if it is properly upheld, it grows throughout the organization gradually. Thus, whether you're starting with one employee or ten, the importance of it doesn't lessen.

Core Values Word Cloud Concept
© *mybaitshop - Fotolia.com*

6. Customer Management

Marketing Strategies:

Marketing is an essential part of your business if you want it to thrive successfully in the market. All around you'll see competition flowing out like lava. Marketing mix includes the factors of the 4P's which helps guide the process of marketing. It includes your product, place, pricing, and promotion.

Marketing Mix Diagram © *LiliWhite - Fotolia.com*

Marketing for your product means to instill a perception of product into the minds of a potential customer. There are definite strategies one should follow which are designed, according to the structure of one's own business. However, a standard procedure describes market segmentation, targeting, positioning, and gaining a competitive advantage. Also, market analysis and customer analysis where you'll be selling your product/service, will contribute into your understanding of how to market your product/service efficaciously. Market segmentation allows a breakdown of the entire market into smaller markets to identify which is the most suitable area for you. Targeting will help focus your business into the prospective customers, only instead of marketing to the whole population, most of whom might be irrelevant to your product; you will market to a certain niche. For example, if you're business relates to teenagers then why market to all the adults and old-aged people out there? Targeting saves you from putting so much money and time in a deep hole of disappointment. Lastly, a competitive advantage is for you to isolate the "big idea" that differentiates your product from others. The only way to outshine your product/service is by displaying the best feature in front of the market with clarity. So once you know what your best selling point is, you would only focus on advertising that to attract the maximum customers.

Great Idea
© *DOC RABE Media - Fotolia.com*

When a target market has been derived, you will have many options to get further ahead in your main marketing objective. There is a different mix of the marketing strategies that you can opt to market your product and disseminate the information of your company into the market. It includes the following: Print media, TV advertising, Telephone, Direct mail, and Internet advertisements. A collective of them could be chosen to mix and match your requirements and needs, keeping in mind the level of investment you have.

Print media which includes flyers, posters, billboards, newspapers, magazines, etc. and TV advertising can be pretty expensive, so most likely not feasible for you, because you're initially starting with a low amount. Nonetheless, Internet, telephone, and direct mail require a very low amount of investment and have the potential to be much more effective if utilized strategically.

Internet is the best tool for marketing, especially on social networking websites such as Facebook and twitter. People have grown rapidly through the use of these websites and are operating online all the way. Just think, how much money do you need to post a page on Facebook? ZERO! Other Internet advertisements include making your own website. Websites can be made at home if you have the knowledge and skills to develop one, otherwise you could hire someone to do the job for you. It doesn't cost a fortune so you don't need to stress much about it.

Pricing Strategies:

Either a product can be distinguished from other products of the same industry or it might be a similar product which already exists in the market and known to all. This difference matters in determining which pricing strategy will be appropriate for your business type.

Cost-plus pricing strategy is the most effective when countering a solution for maximum profit with low investment. The strategy includes calculating the manufacturing cost of the product or the assembling to delivering of the service and then adding a percentage mark-up for profit. This ensures that all of your production cost has been covered and you're making an extra profit on selling of each piece of product or service.

man using calculator © *jeremias münch - Fotolia.com*

Penetration pricing would help you to enter an already established market. The strategy followed in this concept is to state your market price below that of your competitor's price. This would attract the potential customers towards your brand and eventually, when you have developed a brand image, you can increase prices accordingly.

However, if your product is a new concept or invention then you have the leverage to yourself. The strategy of price skimming can be opted if you think that people will see the product/service as an impressive conceptualization. Then you can instantly add a huge mark-up profit to your production price. It will additionally give the image of the brand as a good quality product/service.

Dealing with Competition:

Competition acts as a significant constraint towards your business' success. In fact, if your product is a commercial one there are inelastic factors in which prices are usually the same throughout the city. However, if you're starting a business with a little investment then you must have a competitive advantage, thus making the dealing with the competition a bit easier.

There are strategies to deal with every dilemma that arises in a business and therefore a systematic guideline of how to deal with competitors is also accessible. Firstly, you have to list down all the companies which provide the same product or service that you do, and then analyze their dominance around the market. Look into the pricing strategy, quality levels, and advertising tools. After all the research, brainstorm their individual ideas and analyze why and how each of them have been able to sustain in the market. Use their strengths and weaknesses to your advantage smartly.

If a competitor is giving you a hard time by attracting your customers, you must understand why the customers are willing to go to them instead of being loyal to you. It is essential that you look into your business strategy at the same time to deal with the hindrance smartly. For example, you might have the chance to reach to untapped markets of the competitors where you'll get full opportunity to enhance you product sales.

Marathon, black silhouettes of runners on the sunset
© Andrey Burmakin - Fotolia.com

7. Revenue and Expense Management

Retrieving Revenues:

A company operating without a good margin of revenue is a total failure and no one wants to experience that nightmare in their life. Ensuring that you achieve the maximum revenue is by concentrating on attaining the highest market share possible. The target is obviously not child's play, but is surely possible through effective strategic implementation. This includes marketing, pricing, and dealing with competition strategies. This ensures that more and more customers express loyalty to your brand and gradually the market share escalates. It becomes very hard for those who have more than one identical product in a particular market, because competition is greater. However, the price penetration is usually opted by them to start with lower prices, in order to entice the customers towards the brand. Most of the other companies can maximize their revenues by cutting costs to the least and increasing profit margins to an acceptable range. Pricing strategy often travels in alignment to revenue maximization strategies because the price of a product or service is highly essential in determining the highest level of revenue that can be achieved.

Prioritizing Expenses:

Expenses are the explicit costs of a business which it incurs throughout the operation of the business. It is mandatory to keep these to a minimum due to financial obligations. There will be a large number of expenses incurring, mostly expected ones, but sometimes a few unexpected ones as well. Maintaining a list of all the expenses at regular intervals helps an entrepreneur to interpret costs on a monthly or weekly basis. Out of those listed expenses, once you sit down and comprehend each of them, you'll realize that some expenses are increasing your cost significantly or possibly, they might not even contribute to the profit of a business. The purpose of doing so is to then eliminate all the expenses that you think are superfluous in order for your business to thrive. Consequently, redundancy of expenses will allow flexibility to your price range of the product or service.

Scissors cut business expense costs
© *Michael Brown - Fotolia.com*

To abundantly operate your business under strategic affair, you should rank your expenses in order of priority. Highest priority for a salon business might be the rental place and the equipment required. So whenever you need to cut down a few expenses in the times of a crisis, you can start from the bottom of the list. The ranking can be arranged by scrutinizing the expenses without which your business wouldn't be able to function, even for a day. Moreover, cost versus benefit analysis of the expenses would give you an additional rich picture to help assist the course of prioritizing expenses.

Profit Maximization Strategies:

The ultimate goal of any business or company is attaining an enriching profit that would enhance the business value, and eventually with augmented development, goodwill. Profit maximization strategies aim to raise profits by lowering the costs and increasing the prices, at which the product or service is provided to the customer.

Profit, Loss, Risks Dice Showing Incomes
© *Stuart Miles - Fotolia.com*

The objective is to focus primarily on products that incur the highest income. For example, if you have a catering business and you know that one theme is chosen the most, then only provide that theme instead of all themes which would incur unnecessary cost. A common practiced profit maximization strategy includes the use of pricing strategies to increase the prices to the highest amount possible while keeping in mind the "willingness-to-buy" factor of a consumer. This factor determines how much a customer is willing to pay for a particular product or service. The key is to not just to work hard, but also to work smart.

8. Conclusion

A comprehensive guideline on how to establish a business with low investment has been discussed above, and the most striking fact that you must have noticed, is that most of the strategies include dedicating time, energy, and commitment. This evidently shows that the triumph of a business doesn't rely on how much you invest, but rather how strongly you can stand and survive in the market by working smartly and effectively. However, there obviously are cost-incurring expenses, but the goal is to minimize them with effective brainstorming and evaluating your market and customers. Only with the mixture of all the strategies, will the business grow into the competition with the famous companies known all over the world. This is your chance to become one of the billionaires whose work have inspired you and if you just look around, most of them had also started initially with a low investment on their hands.

Success - Business Concept
© DOC RABE Media - Fotolia.com

Author Bio

Education

Bachelors, Human Resource Management University of the Punjab
2010 - Present
High School, Computer Sciences Forman Christian College
2008 – 2010

Check out some of the other JD-Biz Publishing books

Gardening Series on Amazon

Health Learning Series

Health Learning Series

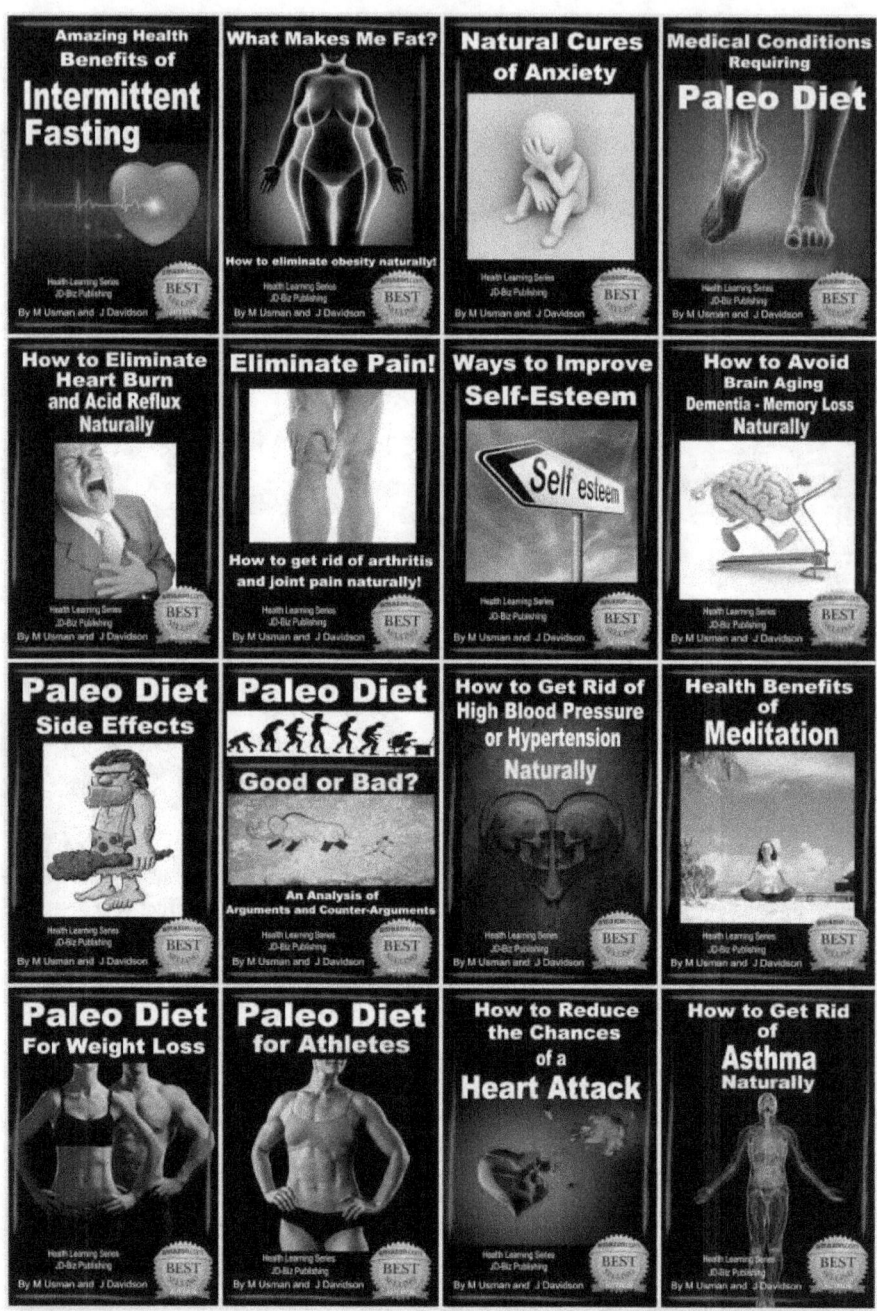

Amazing Animal Book Series

Learn To Draw Series

How to Build and Plan Books

Entrepreneur Book Series

Our books are available at

1. Amazon.com

2. Barnes and Noble

3. Itunes

4. Kobo

5. Smashwords

6. Google Play Books

Publisher

JD-Biz Corp

P O Box 374

Mendon, Utah 84325

http://www.jd-biz.com/

Mendon Cottage Books

P O Box 374, Mendon Utah 84325

www.ingramcontent.com/pod-product-compliance
Lightning Source LLC
Chambersburg PA
CBHW071013180526
45168CB00003B/1400